50 Premium Coffee Recipes for Home

By: Kelly Johnson

Table of Contents

- Espresso Martini
- Affogato al Caffè
- Mocha Java Mousse
- Coffee-Rubbed Ribeye
- Tiramisu
- Cold Brew Coffee Ice Cream
- Coffee-Braised Short Ribs
- Espresso Brownies
- Coffee Cheesecake
- Cappuccino Cupcakes
- Coffee Panna Cotta
- Caramel Coffee Sauce
- Coffee-Glazed Donuts
- Java Almond Cake
- Coffee-Stout BBQ Sauce
- Coffee-Infused Chocolate Truffles
- Coffee Granita
- Coffee and Walnut Bread
- Espresso-Roasted Chickpeas
- Coffee Crème Brûlée
- Coffee-Soaked Pound Cake
- Vietnamese Egg Coffee
- Coffee and Cardamom Cake
- Irish Coffee Cake
- Espresso Poached Pears
- Coffee Ice Cubes
- Hazelnut Coffee Biscotti
- Coffee-Ricotta Fritters
- Coffee-Infused Cream Puffs
- Spiced Coffee Rubbed Chicken
- Coffee Milkshake
- Mocha Macarons

- Coffee Pancakes
- Coffee-Orange Glazed Ham
- Coffee-Infused Caramel Flan
- Espresso-Infused Soufflé
- Coffee-Scented Rice Pudding
- Almond Coffee Cake
- Coffee and Brown Sugar Granola
- Coffee-Infused Beef Stew
- Coffee Almond Ice Cream
- Affogato Cheesecake
- Mocha Bread Pudding
- Coffee-Maple Syrup
- Coffee-Walnut Brownies
- Espresso Trifle
- Coffee-Glazed Chicken Wings
- Mocha Buttercream Frosting
- Espresso Chocolate Sauce
- Coffee Smoothie

Espresso Martini

- 1 shot of freshly brewed espresso
- 1 1/2 oz vodka
- 1 oz coffee liqueur (like Kahlúa)
- 1/2 oz simple syrup (optional, for extra sweetness)
- Ice
- Coffee beans for garnish

Shake all ingredients with ice and strain into a chilled martini glass. Garnish with coffee beans.

Affogato al Caffè

- 1-2 scoops of vanilla ice cream (or gelato)
- 1 shot of hot espresso
- Optional: a splash of liqueur (like Amaretto) for added flavor

Instructions:

1. **Prepare the Espresso:** Brew a fresh shot of espresso.
2. **Scoop the Ice Cream:** Place 1-2 scoops of vanilla ice cream into a serving glass or bowl.
3. **Pour the Espresso:** Immediately pour the hot espresso over the ice cream.
4. **Optional:** Add a splash of liqueur if desired.

Serve immediately, allowing the hot espresso to slightly melt the ice cream, creating a delightful blend of hot and cold.

Mocha Java Mousse

Ingredients:

- 1 cup heavy cream
- 1/2 cup brewed coffee (cooled)
- 1/4 cup cocoa powder
- 1/4 cup granulated sugar
- 3 large egg yolks
- 1/2 cup semisweet chocolate (chopped)
- 1 tsp vanilla extract
- Pinch of salt

Instructions:

1. **Prepare the Chocolate:** Melt the semisweet chocolate in a heatproof bowl over simmering water (double boiler method) or in the microwave in 20-second intervals. Stir until smooth and let it cool slightly.
2. **Whip the Cream:** In a medium bowl, whip the heavy cream until soft peaks form. Set aside.
3. **Mix Cocoa and Coffee:** In another bowl, whisk together the cocoa powder, granulated sugar, and brewed coffee until smooth.
4. **Cook the Egg Yolks:** In a small saucepan over medium heat, gently heat the egg yolks, stirring constantly until slightly thickened. Do not let it boil.
5. **Combine Ingredients:** Remove from heat and whisk in the cooled melted chocolate and vanilla extract. Stir until fully combined.
6. **Fold in the Cream:** Gently fold the whipped cream into the chocolate mixture until well incorporated.
7. **Chill:** Spoon the mousse into individual serving glasses or bowls. Refrigerate for at least 2 hours, or until set.
8. **Serve:** Garnish with chocolate shavings or a dollop of whipped cream if desired.

Enjoy your rich and creamy Mocha Java Mousse!

Coffee-Rubbed Ribeye

Ingredients:

- 2 ribeye steaks (about 1 1/2 inches thick)
- 2 tbsp ground coffee (coarse grind)
- 1 tbsp brown sugar
- 1 tbsp paprika
- 1 tsp garlic powder
- 1 tsp onion powder
- 1/2 tsp black pepper
- 1/2 tsp salt
- 1/2 tsp cayenne pepper (optional, for heat)
- Olive oil (for brushing)

Instructions:

1. **Prepare the Rub:** In a small bowl, mix together ground coffee, brown sugar, paprika, garlic powder, onion powder, black pepper, salt, and cayenne pepper if using.
2. **Season the Steaks:** Pat the ribeye steaks dry with paper towels. Brush both sides with olive oil and then generously rub the coffee mixture onto the steaks.
3. **Rest the Steaks:** Let the steaks sit at room temperature for about 30 minutes to allow the flavors to meld.
4. **Cook:** Preheat your grill or skillet to high heat. Cook the steaks for about 4-5 minutes per side for medium-rare, or to your desired doneness.
5. **Rest and Serve:** Remove the steaks from heat and let them rest for 5 minutes before slicing.

Enjoy your flavorful, coffee-rubbed ribeye!

Tiramisu

Ingredients:

- 6 large egg yolks
- 3/4 cup granulated sugar
- 1 cup mascarpone cheese
- 1 cup heavy cream
- 1 cup strong brewed coffee (cooled)
- 1/4 cup coffee liqueur (optional)
- 24-30 ladyfingers
- Unsweetened cocoa powder (for dusting)

Instructions:

1. **Prepare the Cream Mixture:** Whisk the egg yolks and sugar together until pale and thick. Gradually add mascarpone cheese and mix until smooth.
2. **Whip the Cream:** In a separate bowl, whip the heavy cream until stiff peaks form. Gently fold the whipped cream into the mascarpone mixture.
3. **Coffee Mixture:** Mix the cooled coffee with coffee liqueur if using.
4. **Assemble:** Quickly dip each ladyfinger into the coffee mixture and layer them in the bottom of a dish. Spread half of the mascarpone mixture over the ladyfingers. Repeat with another layer of dipped ladyfingers and top with the remaining mascarpone mixture.
5. **Chill:** Refrigerate for at least 4 hours, or overnight, to allow flavors to meld and the dessert to set.
6. **Serve:** Dust with cocoa powder before serving.

Enjoy your classic, creamy tiramisu!

Cold Brew Coffee Ice Cream

Ingredients:

- 1 cup cold brew coffee (strong and concentrated)
- 1 cup whole milk
- 1 cup heavy cream
- 3/4 cup granulated sugar
- 4 large egg yolks
- 1 tsp vanilla extract
- Pinch of salt

Instructions:

1. **Prepare the Base:** In a medium saucepan, combine the milk, heavy cream, and sugar. Heat over medium heat until the sugar is fully dissolved and the mixture is warm but not boiling.
2. **Temper the Egg Yolks:** In a separate bowl, whisk the egg yolks. Gradually add a small amount of the warm milk mixture to the yolks, whisking constantly to temper them. Once combined, pour the yolk mixture back into the saucepan with the remaining milk mixture.
3. **Cook the Custard:** Cook the mixture over medium heat, stirring constantly, until it thickens slightly and reaches 170-175°F (77-80°C). It should coat the back of a spoon.
4. **Add Coffee and Cool:** Remove the saucepan from heat and stir in the cold brew coffee, vanilla extract, and a pinch of salt. Let the mixture cool to room temperature.
5. **Chill:** Refrigerate the mixture for at least 4 hours or overnight until thoroughly chilled.
6. **Churn:** Pour the chilled mixture into an ice cream maker and churn according to the manufacturer's instructions until it reaches a soft-serve consistency.
7. **Freeze:** Transfer the churned ice cream to a lidded container and freeze for at least 2 hours to firm up.
8. **Serve:** Scoop and enjoy your rich and creamy cold brew coffee ice cream!

Enjoy your coffee-flavored treat!

Coffee-Braised Short Ribs

Ingredients:

- 4 lbs beef short ribs
- Salt and black pepper (to taste)
- 2 tbsp olive oil
- 1 large onion (chopped)
- 3 cloves garlic (minced)
- 2 carrots (chopped)
- 2 celery stalks (chopped)
- 1 cup strong brewed coffee
- 1 cup beef broth
- 1/2 cup red wine (optional)
- 2 tbsp tomato paste
- 2 tbsp brown sugar
- 1 tsp dried thyme
- 1 bay leaf

Instructions:

1. **Preheat Oven:** Preheat your oven to 325°F (165°C).
2. **Season and Sear the Ribs:** Pat the short ribs dry with paper towels. Season generously with salt and black pepper. Heat olive oil in a large ovenproof pot or Dutch oven over medium-high heat. Sear the short ribs on all sides until browned. Remove the ribs and set aside.
3. **Cook the Vegetables:** In the same pot, add the chopped onion, garlic, carrots, and celery. Cook for about 5-7 minutes, or until the vegetables are softened.
4. **Add Liquids and Flavorings:** Stir in the tomato paste and cook for another 2 minutes. Add the brewed coffee, beef broth, red wine (if using), brown sugar, dried thyme, and bay leaf. Stir to combine and bring to a simmer.
5. **Braise:** Return the seared short ribs to the pot, making sure they are submerged in the liquid. Cover the pot with a lid or foil.
6. **Cook in the Oven:** Place the pot in the preheated oven and braise the short ribs for about 2.5 to 3 hours, or until the meat is tender and easily pulls away from the bone.
7. **Finish and Serve:** Remove the pot from the oven. Transfer the short ribs to a serving platter. Skim any excess fat from the surface of the cooking liquid and discard the bay leaf. Reduce the sauce on the stovetop if desired for a thicker consistency. Pour the sauce over the short ribs before serving.

Serve with mashed potatoes, polenta, or crusty bread to soak up the delicious coffee-infused sauce. Enjoy your flavorful and tender coffee-braised short ribs!

Espresso Brownies

Ingredients:

- 1/2 cup (1 stick) unsalted butter
- 1 cup granulated sugar
- 2 large eggs
- 1 tsp vanilla extract
- 1/2 cup cocoa powder
- 1/2 cup all-purpose flour
- 1/4 tsp salt
- 1/4 tsp baking powder
- 2 tbsp finely ground espresso or instant coffee
- 1/2 cup semisweet chocolate chips (optional)

Instructions:

1. **Preheat Oven:** Preheat your oven to 350°F (175°C). Grease or line an 8x8-inch baking pan with parchment paper.
2. **Melt Butter:** In a medium saucepan, melt the butter over low heat. Remove from heat and stir in the sugar, eggs, and vanilla extract.
3. **Mix Dry Ingredients:** Stir in cocoa powder, flour, salt, and baking powder. Mix until just combined. Fold in the ground espresso or instant coffee. If using, fold in the chocolate chips.
4. **Bake:** Pour the batter into the prepared pan and spread evenly. Bake for 20-25 minutes, or until a toothpick inserted into the center comes out with a few moist crumbs.
5. **Cool:** Allow the brownies to cool in the pan before cutting into squares.

Enjoy your rich, coffee-infused brownies!

Coffee Cheesecake

Ingredients:

Crust:

- 1 1/2 cups graham cracker crumbs
- 1/4 cup granulated sugar
- 1/2 cup unsalted butter (melted)

Filling:

- 4 (8 oz) packages cream cheese (softened)
- 1 cup granulated sugar
- 1 cup sour cream
- 1 cup heavy cream
- 3 large eggs
- 1 cup brewed coffee (cooled)
- 1 tsp vanilla extract

Topping (optional):

- Whipped cream
- Cocoa powder or chocolate shavings

Instructions:

1. **Preheat Oven:** Preheat your oven to 325°F (165°C). Grease a 9-inch springform pan.
2. **Prepare Crust:** In a bowl, mix graham cracker crumbs, sugar, and melted butter. Press the mixture into the bottom of the prepared pan to form an even layer. Bake for 10 minutes, then let cool.
3. **Prepare Filling:** Beat the cream cheese and sugar together until smooth. Add sour cream, heavy cream, coffee, and vanilla extract. Beat until fully combined. Add eggs one at a time, mixing on low speed after each addition.
4. **Bake:** Pour the filling over the cooled crust. Tap the pan gently to release air bubbles. Bake for 50-60 minutes, or until the center is set but still slightly jiggly.
5. **Cool:** Turn off the oven and let the cheesecake cool inside with the door ajar for 1 hour. Remove and refrigerate for at least 4 hours, or overnight.
6. **Serve:** Top with whipped cream and cocoa powder or chocolate shavings if desired.

Enjoy your creamy coffee cheesecake!

Cappuccino Cupcakes

Ingredients:

Cupcakes:

- 1 1/2 cups all-purpose flour
- 1 cup granulated sugar
- 1/2 cup unsalted butter (softened)
- 1/2 cup brewed espresso (cooled)
- 1/4 cup milk
- 2 large eggs
- 1 1/2 tsp baking powder
- 1/2 tsp baking soda
- 1/4 tsp salt
- 1 tsp vanilla extract

Frosting:

- 1/2 cup unsalted butter (softened)
- 2 cups powdered sugar
- 2 tbsp brewed espresso (cooled)
- 1 tbsp milk
- 1/2 tsp vanilla extract

Instructions:

1. **Preheat Oven:** Preheat your oven to 350°F (175°C). Line a muffin tin with paper liners.
2. **Prepare Cupcake Batter:** In a bowl, mix flour, baking powder, baking soda, and salt. In a separate bowl, beat the butter and sugar until light and fluffy. Add eggs one at a time, then vanilla extract. Mix in the espresso and milk alternately with the dry ingredients until just combined.
3. **Bake:** Divide the batter evenly among the cupcake liners. Bake for 18-22 minutes, or until a toothpick inserted into the center comes out clean. Let cool completely on a wire rack.
4. **Prepare Frosting:** Beat the butter until creamy. Gradually add powdered sugar, espresso, milk, and vanilla, beating until smooth and fluffy.
5. **Frost:** Pipe or spread the frosting onto the cooled cupcakes.

Enjoy your delightful cappuccino cupcakes!

Coffee Panna Cotta

Ingredients:

- 1 cup heavy cream
- 1 cup whole milk
- 1/2 cup granulated sugar
- 2 tbsp instant coffee granules or finely ground espresso
- 2 1/2 tsp unflavored gelatin (about 1 packet)
- 1/4 cup water
- 1 tsp vanilla extract

Instructions:

1. **Prepare Gelatin:** In a small bowl, sprinkle the gelatin over the water and let it sit for 5 minutes to bloom.
2. **Heat Cream Mixture:** In a saucepan, combine the heavy cream, milk, and sugar. Heat over medium heat until the sugar dissolves and the mixture is warm but not boiling. Stir in the instant coffee until fully dissolved.
3. **Dissolve Gelatin:** Remove the saucepan from heat and stir in the bloomed gelatin until completely dissolved. Mix in the vanilla extract.
4. **Pour and Chill:** Pour the mixture into individual serving glasses or ramekins. Refrigerate for at least 4 hours or until set.
5. **Serve:** Garnish with whipped cream or a dusting of cocoa powder if desired.

Enjoy your creamy coffee panna cotta!

Caramel Coffee Sauce

Ingredients:

- 1 cup granulated sugar
- 6 tbsp unsalted butter
- 1/2 cup heavy cream
- 1/4 cup brewed coffee (hot)
- 1/2 tsp vanilla extract
- Pinch of salt

Instructions:

1. **Caramelize Sugar:** In a medium saucepan over medium heat, melt the sugar, stirring constantly until it turns a deep amber color.
2. **Add Butter:** Carefully add the butter, stirring until melted and combined with the caramelized sugar.
3. **Add Cream and Coffee:** Slowly whisk in the hot cream and brewed coffee. Continue to cook, stirring, until smooth and thickened.
4. **Finish:** Remove from heat and stir in vanilla extract and a pinch of salt.
5. **Cool and Store:** Allow the sauce to cool slightly before using. Store in an airtight container in the refrigerator for up to two weeks. Reheat before using.

Enjoy drizzling this rich caramel coffee sauce over desserts or ice cream!

Coffee-Glazed Donuts

Ingredients:

For the Donuts:

- 2 1/4 cups all-purpose flour
- 1/2 cup granulated sugar
- 1/4 cup packed brown sugar
- 2 1/2 tsp baking powder
- 1/2 tsp salt
- 1/2 tsp ground cinnamon
- 1/2 cup whole milk
- 1/4 cup brewed coffee (cooled)
- 1/4 cup unsalted butter (melted)
- 2 large eggs
- 1 tsp vanilla extract

For the Coffee Glaze:

- 1 cup powdered sugar
- 2 tbsp brewed coffee (cooled)
- 1-2 tbsp milk (if needed to adjust consistency)
- 1/2 tsp vanilla extract

Instructions:

1. **Preheat Oven:** Preheat your oven to 375°F (190°C). Grease or line a donut pan.
2. **Mix Dry Ingredients:** In a large bowl, whisk together flour, granulated sugar, brown sugar, baking powder, salt, and cinnamon.
3. **Mix Wet Ingredients:** In another bowl, whisk together milk, coffee, melted butter, eggs, and vanilla extract.
4. **Combine:** Pour the wet ingredients into the dry ingredients and stir until just combined.
5. **Fill Pan:** Spoon or pipe the batter into the donut pan, filling each cavity about 2/3 full.
6. **Bake:** Bake for 10-12 minutes, or until a toothpick inserted into the center comes out clean. Let cool slightly before glazing.
7. **Prepare Glaze:** In a small bowl, whisk together powdered sugar, brewed coffee, milk (if needed), and vanilla extract until smooth. Adjust the consistency with more milk if necessary.
8. **Glaze Donuts:** Dip the top of each donut into the coffee glaze and let the excess drip off. Place the donuts on a wire rack to let the glaze set.

Enjoy your freshly baked coffee-glazed donuts!

Java Almond Cake

Ingredients:

- 1 cup almond flour
- 1 cup all-purpose flour
- 1 cup granulated sugar
- 1/2 cup unsalted butter (softened)
- 3 large eggs
- 1/2 cup brewed coffee (cooled)
- 1/4 cup milk
- 1 tsp vanilla extract
- 1/2 tsp almond extract
- 1 1/2 tsp baking powder
- 1/4 tsp salt

Instructions:

1. **Preheat Oven:** Preheat your oven to 350°F (175°C). Grease and flour an 8-inch round cake pan or line it with parchment paper.
2. **Mix Dry Ingredients:** In a bowl, combine almond flour, all-purpose flour, baking powder, and salt.
3. **Cream Butter and Sugar:** In a large bowl, beat the butter and granulated sugar until light and fluffy.
4. **Add Eggs:** Add the eggs one at a time, beating well after each addition. Stir in vanilla and almond extracts.
5. **Combine Wet and Dry:** Gradually mix in the dry ingredients, alternating with the brewed coffee and milk, until just combined.
6. **Bake:** Pour the batter into the prepared pan and smooth the top. Bake for 25-30 minutes, or until a toothpick inserted into the center comes out clean.
7. **Cool and Serve:** Allow the cake to cool in the pan for 10 minutes before transferring to a wire rack to cool completely.

Enjoy your moist and flavorful Java Almond Cake!

Coffee-Stout BBQ Sauce

Ingredients:

- 1 cup stout beer (such as Guinness)
- 1 cup brewed coffee
- 1 cup ketchup
- 1/2 cup brown sugar
- 1/4 cup apple cider vinegar
- 2 tbsp Worcestershire sauce
- 2 tbsp soy sauce
- 1 tbsp Dijon mustard
- 2 cloves garlic (minced)
- 1 small onion (finely chopped)
- 1/2 tsp smoked paprika
- 1/2 tsp ground cumin
- 1/4 tsp black pepper
- 1/4 tsp salt
- 1/4 tsp red pepper flakes (optional, for heat)

Instructions:

1. **Cook Aromatics:** In a medium saucepan over medium heat, sauté the chopped onion and minced garlic in a bit of oil until softened, about 5 minutes.
2. **Combine Ingredients:** Add the stout beer, brewed coffee, ketchup, brown sugar, apple cider vinegar, Worcestershire sauce, soy sauce, Dijon mustard, smoked paprika, cumin, black pepper, salt, and red pepper flakes (if using).
3. **Simmer:** Bring the mixture to a boil, then reduce the heat and let it simmer, uncovered, for about 20-30 minutes, or until the sauce has thickened to your desired consistency. Stir occasionally.
4. **Adjust Seasoning:** Taste the sauce and adjust seasoning as needed.
5. **Cool and Store:** Let the sauce cool to room temperature. Store in an airtight container in the refrigerator for up to 2 weeks.

This rich and flavorful Coffee-Stout BBQ Sauce is perfect for grilling or as a marinade. Enjoy!

Coffee-Infused Chocolate Truffles

Ingredients:

- 8 oz semisweet or dark chocolate (chopped)
- 1/2 cup heavy cream
- 2 tbsp brewed coffee (strong)
- 1 tbsp unsalted butter
- Cocoa powder (for rolling)
- Optional: finely ground coffee or chopped nuts (for coating)

Instructions:

1. **Heat Cream:** In a small saucepan, heat the heavy cream over medium heat until it just begins to simmer.
2. **Add Coffee:** Stir in the brewed coffee and unsalted butter.
3. **Melt Chocolate:** Place the chopped chocolate in a heatproof bowl. Pour the hot cream mixture over the chocolate and let it sit for 2-3 minutes. Stir until the chocolate is completely melted and smooth.
4. **Chill Ganache:** Refrigerate the mixture for about 1-2 hours, or until firm enough to scoop.
5. **Form Truffles:** Using a small scoop or spoon, form the ganache into small balls. Roll each ball in cocoa powder, or if desired, finely ground coffee or chopped nuts.
6. **Store:** Keep the truffles in an airtight container in the refrigerator. Let them come to room temperature before serving for the best flavor.

Enjoy your rich, coffee-infused chocolate truffles!

Coffee Granita

Ingredients:

- 2 cups brewed coffee (strong and cooled)
- 1/2 cup granulated sugar
- 1/4 cup water
- 1 tsp vanilla extract (optional)

Instructions:

1. **Prepare the Syrup:** In a small saucepan, combine the sugar and water. Heat over medium heat, stirring until the sugar is completely dissolved. Let the syrup cool to room temperature.
2. **Combine Coffee and Syrup:** Stir the cooled syrup into the brewed coffee. If using, add vanilla extract and mix well.
3. **Freeze:** Pour the coffee mixture into a shallow baking dish or pan.
4. **Scrape:** After about 1-2 hours, use a fork to scrape and stir the mixture. Continue to freeze and scrape every 30 minutes until the granita is fully frozen and has a fluffy, crystalline texture. This process usually takes about 4-6 hours.
5. **Serve:** Spoon the granita into glasses or bowls and serve immediately. You can garnish with a dollop of whipped cream or a sprinkle of chocolate shavings if desired.

Enjoy your refreshing Coffee Granita!

Coffee and Walnut Bread

Ingredients:

- 1/2 cup brewed coffee (cooled)
- 1/2 cup unsalted butter (softened)
- 1 cup granulated sugar
- 2 large eggs
- 1 tsp vanilla extract
- 1 1/2 cups all-purpose flour
- 1 tsp baking powder
- 1/2 tsp baking soda
- 1/4 tsp salt
- 1 cup walnuts (chopped)

Instructions:

1. **Preheat Oven:** Preheat your oven to 350°F (175°C). Grease and flour a 9x5-inch loaf pan.
2. **Prepare Wet Ingredients:** In a bowl, cream together the softened butter and sugar until light and fluffy. Beat in the eggs, one at a time, then add the vanilla extract.
3. **Combine Wet and Dry:** In a separate bowl, whisk together the flour, baking powder, baking soda, and salt. Gradually add the dry ingredients to the wet ingredients, alternating with the brewed coffee. Mix until just combined.
4. **Add Walnuts:** Fold in the chopped walnuts.
5. **Bake:** Pour the batter into the prepared loaf pan. Bake for 50-60 minutes, or until a toothpick inserted into the center comes out clean.
6. **Cool:** Allow the bread to cool in the pan for 10 minutes before transferring to a wire rack to cool completely.

Enjoy your coffee and walnut bread, perfect for breakfast or a snack!

Espresso-Roasted Chickpeas

Ingredients:

- 1 can (15 oz) chickpeas (rinsed and drained)
- 1 tbsp olive oil
- 1 tbsp finely ground espresso or instant coffee
- 1 tsp smoked paprika
- 1/2 tsp garlic powder
- 1/2 tsp onion powder
- 1/4 tsp salt
- 1/4 tsp black pepper

Instructions:

1. **Preheat Oven:** Preheat your oven to 400°F (200°C). Line a baking sheet with parchment paper.
2. **Prepare Chickpeas:** Pat the chickpeas dry with paper towels. Remove any loose skins if desired.
3. **Season:** In a bowl, toss the chickpeas with olive oil, ground espresso, smoked paprika, garlic powder, onion powder, salt, and pepper until evenly coated.
4. **Roast:** Spread the chickpeas in a single layer on the prepared baking sheet. Roast for 25-30 minutes, shaking the pan halfway through, until crispy and golden.
5. **Cool:** Let the chickpeas cool completely before serving. They will become crispier as they cool.

Enjoy your crunchy, coffee-flavored snack!

Coffee Crème Brûlée

Ingredients:

- 2 cups heavy cream
- 1/2 cup brewed coffee (strong and cooled)
- 5 large egg yolks
- 1/2 cup granulated sugar (plus extra for caramelizing)
- 1 tsp vanilla extract
- Pinch of salt

Instructions:

1. **Preheat Oven:** Preheat your oven to 325°F (165°C). Place 4-6 ramekins in a baking dish.
2. **Heat Cream:** In a saucepan, heat the heavy cream over medium heat until it begins to steam. Do not let it boil. Remove from heat and stir in the brewed coffee.
3. **Prepare Egg Mixture:** In a bowl, whisk together the egg yolks, sugar, vanilla extract, and a pinch of salt until well combined and slightly thickened.
4. **Combine:** Gradually add the hot cream mixture to the egg mixture, whisking constantly to temper the eggs. Strain the mixture through a fine-mesh sieve into a clean bowl or measuring cup to remove any curdled bits.
5. **Fill Ramekins:** Pour the custard mixture evenly into the ramekins.
6. **Bake:** Place the baking dish in the oven and carefully pour hot water into the dish around the ramekins, creating a water bath that reaches halfway up the sides of the ramekins. Bake for 35-45 minutes, or until the custards are set but still slightly jiggly in the center.
7. **Cool:** Remove the ramekins from the water bath and let them cool to room temperature. Refrigerate for at least 2 hours or until fully chilled.
8. **Caramelize Sugar:** Before serving, sprinkle a thin, even layer of granulated sugar over each custard. Using a kitchen torch, caramelize the sugar until it melts and turns golden brown. If you don't have a torch, you can place the ramekins under a broiler for a minute or two, but watch carefully to avoid burning.

Enjoy your creamy, coffee-flavored crème brûlée with its crispy caramelized top!

Coffee-Soaked Pound Cake

Ingredients:

For the Pound Cake:

- 1 cup unsalted butter (softened)
- 1 cup granulated sugar
- 4 large eggs
- 1 1/2 cups all-purpose flour
- 1/2 tsp baking powder
- 1/4 tsp salt
- 1/2 cup brewed coffee (cooled)
- 1 tsp vanilla extract

For the Coffee Soak:

- 1/2 cup brewed coffee (cooled)
- 1/4 cup granulated sugar

Instructions:

1. **Preheat Oven:** Preheat your oven to 350°F (175°C). Grease and flour a loaf pan.
2. **Prepare Cake Batter:** In a large bowl, cream together the softened butter and sugar until light and fluffy. Beat in the eggs one at a time. Add the vanilla extract.
3. **Combine Dry Ingredients:** In a separate bowl, whisk together the flour, baking powder, and salt. Gradually add the dry ingredients to the butter mixture, alternating with the brewed coffee, until just combined.
4. **Bake:** Pour the batter into the prepared loaf pan and smooth the top. Bake for 50-60 minutes, or until a toothpick inserted into the center comes out clean.
5. **Cool and Soak:** Let the cake cool in the pan for 10 minutes, then transfer it to a wire rack. In a small bowl, mix the remaining brewed coffee with the granulated sugar until the sugar dissolves. While the cake is still warm, brush or pour the coffee mixture over the top, allowing it to soak in.
6. **Serve:** Allow the cake to cool completely before slicing and serving.

Enjoy your moist and flavorful coffee-soaked pound cake!

Vietnamese Egg Coffee

Ingredients:

- 1/2 cup strong brewed Vietnamese coffee or espresso
- 2 large egg yolks
- 1/2 cup sweetened condensed milk
- 1/2 tsp vanilla extract
- Cocoa powder or ground coffee (for garnish, optional)

Instructions:

1. **Brew Coffee:** Prepare your strong Vietnamese coffee or espresso and set aside.
2. **Make Egg Mixture:** In a heatproof bowl, whisk the egg yolks until frothy. Gradually whisk in the sweetened condensed milk and vanilla extract until well combined and slightly thickened.
3. **Heat Egg Mixture:** Place the bowl over a pot of simmering water (double boiler) and gently heat the mixture while whisking continuously until it's warm and frothy but not cooked.
4. **Combine and Serve:** Pour the hot coffee into a cup. Spoon the frothy egg mixture over the coffee.
5. **Garnish:** Dust with cocoa powder or a pinch of ground coffee if desired.

Enjoy this rich and creamy Vietnamese Egg Coffee!

Coffee and Cardamom Cake

Ingredients:

- 1 1/2 cups all-purpose flour
- 1 cup granulated sugar
- 1/2 cup unsalted butter (softened)
- 1/2 cup brewed coffee (cooled)
- 1/4 cup milk
- 2 large eggs
- 1 tsp baking powder
- 1/2 tsp baking soda
- 1/2 tsp ground cardamom
- 1/4 tsp salt
- 1 tsp vanilla extract

Instructions:

1. **Preheat Oven:** Preheat your oven to 350°F (175°C). Grease and flour an 8-inch round or square cake pan.
2. **Prepare Dry Ingredients:** In a bowl, whisk together flour, baking powder, baking soda, cardamom, and salt.
3. **Cream Butter and Sugar:** In a large bowl, cream together the softened butter and sugar until light and fluffy. Add the eggs one at a time, beating well after each addition. Stir in the vanilla extract.
4. **Combine Wet and Dry:** Gradually mix the dry ingredients into the butter mixture, alternating with the brewed coffee and milk, until just combined.
5. **Bake:** Pour the batter into the prepared pan and smooth the top. Bake for 25-30 minutes, or until a toothpick inserted into the center comes out clean.
6. **Cool and Serve:** Allow the cake to cool in the pan for 10 minutes, then transfer to a wire rack to cool completely.

Enjoy your aromatic Coffee and Cardamom Cake!

Irish Coffee Cake

Ingredients:

For the Cake:

- 1 1/2 cups all-purpose flour
- 1 cup granulated sugar
- 1/2 cup unsalted butter (softened)
- 1/2 cup brewed strong coffee (cooled)
- 1/4 cup Irish whiskey
- 2 large eggs
- 1 tsp baking powder
- 1/2 tsp baking soda
- 1/4 tsp salt
- 1 tsp vanilla extract

For the Coffee Glaze:

- 1/2 cup powdered sugar
- 2 tbsp brewed coffee (cooled)
- 1 tbsp Irish whiskey (optional)

Instructions:

1. **Preheat Oven:** Preheat your oven to 350°F (175°C). Grease and flour an 8-inch round or square cake pan.
2. **Prepare Dry Ingredients:** In a bowl, whisk together flour, baking powder, baking soda, and salt.
3. **Cream Butter and Sugar:** In a large bowl, beat the butter and sugar until light and fluffy. Add the eggs one at a time, beating well after each addition. Mix in the vanilla extract.
4. **Combine Wet and Dry:** Gradually add the dry ingredients to the butter mixture, alternating with the brewed coffee and Irish whiskey, until just combined.
5. **Bake:** Pour the batter into the prepared pan and smooth the top. Bake for 25-30 minutes, or until a toothpick inserted into the center comes out clean.
6. **Prepare Glaze:** While the cake is baking, mix the powdered sugar, brewed coffee, and Irish whiskey (if using) in a small bowl until smooth.
7. **Cool and Glaze:** Allow the cake to cool in the pan for 10 minutes before transferring to a wire rack. Drizzle the coffee glaze over the cooled cake.

Enjoy your flavorful Irish Coffee Cake!

Espresso Poached Pears

Ingredients:

- 4 ripe but firm pears (such as Bosc or Anjou)
- 1 cup brewed espresso (or strong coffee)
- 1 cup water
- 1/2 cup granulated sugar
- 1/4 cup honey
- 1 cinnamon stick
- 2-3 whole cloves
- 1 star anise (optional)
- 1 tsp vanilla extract
- 1 tbsp lemon juice

Instructions:

1. **Prepare Pears:** Peel the pears, leaving the stems intact. Cut a small slice from the bottom of each pear to help them stand upright during poaching.
2. **Prepare Poaching Liquid:** In a saucepan, combine the brewed espresso, water, sugar, honey, cinnamon stick, cloves, star anise (if using), vanilla extract, and lemon juice. Stir to dissolve the sugar.
3. **Poach Pears:** Bring the mixture to a simmer over medium heat. Carefully add the pears to the saucepan, ensuring they are mostly submerged. Simmer gently for 20-30 minutes, or until the pears are tender but still hold their shape. Turn the pears occasionally to ensure even cooking.
4. **Cool:** Once the pears are tender, remove them from the poaching liquid and let them cool to room temperature.
5. **Reduce Poaching Liquid:** Continue to simmer the poaching liquid until it reduces and thickens into a syrup, about 10-15 minutes.
6. **Serve:** Arrange the pears on serving plates and drizzle with the reduced espresso syrup.

Enjoy your elegant and flavorful Espresso Poached Pears!

Coffee Ice Cubes

Ingredients:

- Brewed coffee (cooled)

Instructions:

1. **Brew Coffee:** Brew a strong pot of coffee and let it cool to room temperature. For a more intense flavor, consider using espresso.
2. **Pour into Tray:** Pour the cooled coffee into an ice cube tray.
3. **Freeze:** Place the tray in the freezer and freeze until the coffee is solid, typically about 4-6 hours or overnight.
4. **Store:** Once frozen, you can transfer the coffee cubes to a zip-top bag or airtight container for longer storage. This way, you can easily grab a few cubes whenever needed.

Usage Tips:

- **For Coffee Drinks:** Add coffee cubes to your iced coffee or cold brew to keep it chilled without diluting the flavor.
- **For Smoothies:** Use coffee ice cubes in smoothies for an extra coffee kick.
- **For Baking or Cooking:** Coffee ice cubes can be blended into batters or sauces for added flavor.

Enjoy your perfectly chilled coffee drinks with these easy-to-make coffee ice cubes!

Hazelnut Coffee Biscotti

Ingredients:

- 1 cup hazelnuts (toasted and chopped)
- 2 cups all-purpose flour
- 1 cup granulated sugar
- 1/2 cup brewed coffee (cooled)
- 1/4 cup unsalted butter (softened)
- 3 large eggs
- 1 tsp vanilla extract
- 1 tsp baking powder
- 1/2 tsp baking soda
- 1/4 tsp salt

Instructions:

1. **Preheat Oven:** Preheat your oven to 350°F (175°C). Line a baking sheet with parchment paper.
2. **Mix Wet Ingredients:** In a large bowl, cream together the softened butter and sugar until light and fluffy. Beat in the eggs one at a time, then stir in the vanilla extract and cooled coffee.
3. **Combine Dry Ingredients:** In a separate bowl, whisk together flour, baking powder, baking soda, and salt.
4. **Combine All Ingredients:** Gradually mix the dry ingredients into the wet ingredients until just combined. Fold in the chopped hazelnuts.
5. **Form Dough:** Divide the dough in half and shape each portion into a log about 12 inches long and 2 inches wide on the prepared baking sheet. Flatten the logs slightly.
6. **Bake:** Bake for 25-30 minutes, or until golden and firm. Let the logs cool on the baking sheet for 10 minutes.
7. **Slice and Bake Again:** Transfer the logs to a cutting board and slice them diagonally into 1/2-inch wide pieces. Arrange the slices cut side down on the baking sheet. Bake for an additional 10-15 minutes, flipping halfway through, until crisp.
8. **Cool:** Let the biscotti cool completely on a wire rack before serving.

Enjoy your crunchy and flavorful Hazelnut Coffee Biscotti with a cup of coffee!

Coffee-Ricotta Fritters

Ingredients:

- 1 cup ricotta cheese
- 1/2 cup all-purpose flour
- 1/4 cup granulated sugar
- 1/4 cup brewed coffee (cooled)
- 1 large egg
- 1 tsp vanilla extract
- 1/2 tsp baking powder
- Pinch of salt
- Vegetable oil (for frying)
- Powdered sugar (for dusting)

Instructions:

1. **Prepare Batter:** In a bowl, mix together ricotta cheese, flour, granulated sugar, brewed coffee, egg, vanilla extract, baking powder, and a pinch of salt until smooth.
2. **Heat Oil:** In a large skillet or deep fryer, heat about 2 inches of vegetable oil to 350°F (175°C).
3. **Fry Fritters:** Drop spoonfuls of the batter into the hot oil, frying in batches to avoid overcrowding. Cook for about 2-3 minutes per side, or until golden brown and puffed. Use a slotted spoon to transfer the fritters to a paper towel-lined plate to drain.
4. **Dust and Serve:** Once drained, dust the fritters with powdered sugar before serving.

Enjoy your light and fluffy Coffee-Ricotta Fritters!

Coffee-Infused Cream Puffs

Ingredients:

For the Choux Pastry:

- 1/2 cup unsalted butter
- 1/2 cup water
- 1/4 cup brewed coffee (cooled)
- 1/2 cup all-purpose flour
- 1/4 tsp salt
- 2 large eggs

For the Coffee Pastry Cream:

- 1 cup whole milk
- 1/2 cup brewed coffee (cooled)
- 1/2 cup granulated sugar
- 3 large egg yolks
- 2 tbsp cornstarch
- 2 tbsp unsalted butter
- 1 tsp vanilla extract

Instructions:

1. **Prepare Choux Pastry:**
    - Preheat your oven to 375°F (190°C) and line a baking sheet with parchment paper.
    - In a saucepan, bring the butter, water, and brewed coffee to a boil. Remove from heat and stir in the flour and salt until combined. Return to low heat and stir for 1-2 minutes to dry out the dough slightly.
    - Transfer the dough to a bowl and let it cool slightly. Beat in the eggs one at a time until the dough is smooth and glossy.
    - Using a pastry bag or spoon, pipe or spoon small mounds of dough onto the prepared baking sheet. Bake for 20-25 minutes, or until puffed and golden. Let cool on a wire rack.
2. **Prepare Coffee Pastry Cream:**
    - In a saucepan, heat the milk and brewed coffee until just boiling. Remove from heat.
    - In a bowl, whisk together the sugar, egg yolks, and cornstarch until smooth. Gradually whisk in the hot milk mixture.
    - Return the mixture to the saucepan and cook over medium heat, stirring constantly until thickened and boiling. Remove from heat and stir in the butter and vanilla extract.

- Transfer the pastry cream to a bowl, cover with plastic wrap (pressing the wrap directly on the surface of the cream to prevent a skin from forming), and chill until cold.

3. **Assemble Cream Puffs:**
    - Once the choux puffs are completely cooled, cut a small slit or remove the tops. Fill each puff with the chilled coffee pastry cream using a pastry bag.

Enjoy your delicious Coffee-Infused Cream Puffs!

Spiced Coffee Rubbed Chicken

Ingredients:

- 4 boneless, skinless chicken breasts (or thighs)
- 2 tbsp ground coffee (medium or coarse grind)
- 1 tbsp paprika
- 1 tbsp brown sugar
- 1 tsp ground cumin
- 1 tsp garlic powder
- 1 tsp onion powder
- 1/2 tsp ground cinnamon
- 1/2 tsp ground coriander
- 1/2 tsp salt
- 1/2 tsp black pepper
- 1 tbsp olive oil (for cooking)

Instructions:

1. **Prepare Spice Rub:** In a small bowl, combine the ground coffee, paprika, brown sugar, cumin, garlic powder, onion powder, cinnamon, coriander, salt, and black pepper. Mix well.
2. **Season Chicken:** Pat the chicken breasts dry with paper towels. Rub the spice mixture evenly over both sides of each chicken breast.
3. **Heat Oil:** Heat olive oil in a large skillet over medium heat.
4. **Cook Chicken:** Add the spiced chicken breasts to the skillet. Cook for 6-8 minutes per side, or until the chicken is cooked through and reaches an internal temperature of 165°F (74°C). The chicken should have a nice sear and the spices should form a flavorful crust.
5. **Rest and Serve:** Transfer the chicken to a plate and let it rest for a few minutes before slicing.

Enjoy your flavorful Spiced Coffee-Rubbed Chicken!

Coffee Milkshake

Ingredients:

- 1 cup brewed coffee (cooled)
- 1 cup vanilla ice cream
- 1/2 cup milk (or more for desired consistency)
- 2 tbsp chocolate syrup or coffee syrup (optional, for extra flavor)
- Whipped cream (for topping, optional)
- Chocolate shavings or coffee beans (for garnish, optional)

Instructions:

1. **Blend Ingredients:** In a blender, combine the cooled brewed coffee, vanilla ice cream, milk, and chocolate syrup (if using). Blend until smooth and creamy. Adjust the milk if you prefer a thinner or thicker consistency.
2. **Serve:** Pour the milkshake into a glass.
3. **Garnish:** Top with whipped cream and garnish with chocolate shavings or coffee beans if desired.
4. **Enjoy:** Serve immediately with a straw or spoon.

Enjoy your creamy and delicious Coffee Milkshake!

Mocha Macarons

Ingredients:

For the Macaron Shells:

- 1 cup powdered sugar
- 1/2 cup almond flour
- 2 large egg whites
- 1/4 tsp cream of tartar
- 1/4 cup granulated sugar
- 1 tbsp cocoa powder
- 1 tsp instant coffee granules (dissolved in 1 tsp hot water)

For the Mocha Filling:

- 1/2 cup unsalted butter (softened)
- 1 cup powdered sugar
- 1 tbsp cocoa powder
- 1 tbsp brewed coffee (cooled)
- 1 tsp vanilla extract

Instructions:

1. **Prepare Shells:**
   - Preheat your oven to 300°F (150°C) and line a baking sheet with parchment paper or a silicone mat.
   - In a bowl, sift together powdered sugar, almond flour, and cocoa powder. Set aside.
   - In a clean bowl, beat egg whites and cream of tartar until soft peaks form. Gradually add granulated sugar, continuing to beat until stiff peaks form.
   - Fold the dry ingredients and coffee mixture into the meringue in thirds, gently folding until fully combined and the batter flows in a ribbon-like consistency.
   - Transfer the batter to a piping bag fitted with a round tip. Pipe small circles onto the prepared baking sheet, spacing them about 1 inch apart. Tap the baking sheet on the counter to release air bubbles and flatten the tops.
2. **Bake:**
   - Bake for 15-18 minutes, or until the macarons have formed a shell and can be easily lifted off the parchment paper.
   - Allow the macarons to cool completely on the baking sheet before removing.
3. **Prepare Filling:**
   - In a bowl, beat the softened butter until creamy. Gradually add powdered sugar and cocoa powder, beating until smooth.
   - Mix in the brewed coffee and vanilla extract until well combined.

4. **Assemble:**
    - Pipe a small amount of mocha filling onto the flat side of one macaron shell. Top with another shell to create a sandwich. Press gently to spread the filling evenly.
5. **Rest and Serve:**
    - Let the assembled macarons rest in an airtight container in the refrigerator for at least 24 hours to allow the flavors to meld.

Enjoy your delightful Mocha Macarons!

Coffee Pancakes

Ingredients:

- 1 cup all-purpose flour
- 2 tbsp granulated sugar
- 1 tbsp baking powder
- 1/4 tsp salt
- 1 cup brewed coffee (cooled)
- 1/4 cup milk
- 1 large egg
- 2 tbsp melted butter (plus more for cooking)
- 1 tsp vanilla extract

Instructions:

1. **Mix Dry Ingredients:** In a large bowl, whisk together flour, sugar, baking powder, and salt.
2. **Combine Wet Ingredients:** In another bowl, mix the brewed coffee, milk, egg, melted butter, and vanilla extract.
3. **Combine and Stir:** Pour the wet ingredients into the dry ingredients and stir until just combined. The batter should be lumpy; avoid overmixing.
4. **Heat Skillet:** Heat a non-stick skillet or griddle over medium heat and lightly grease with butter.
5. **Cook Pancakes:** Pour 1/4 cup of batter onto the skillet for each pancake. Cook until bubbles form on the surface, then flip and cook until golden brown on the other side.
6. **Serve:** Serve warm with your favorite toppings like maple syrup or whipped cream.

Enjoy your flavorful Coffee Pancakes!

Coffee-Orange Glazed Ham

Ingredients:

- 1 fully cooked bone-in ham (about 8-10 lbs)
- 1 cup brewed coffee
- 1/2 cup orange juice
- 1/2 cup brown sugar
- 1/4 cup honey
- 2 tbsp Dijon mustard
- 1 tbsp soy sauce
- 1/2 tsp ground cinnamon
- 1/4 tsp ground cloves
- 1/4 tsp ground allspice
- 2 tbsp cornstarch (optional, for thickening)

Instructions:

1. **Preheat Oven:** Preheat your oven to 325°F (165°C).
2. **Prepare Ham:** Score the surface of the ham in a diamond pattern. Place the ham in a roasting pan.
3. **Make Glaze:** In a saucepan, combine the brewed coffee, orange juice, brown sugar, honey, Dijon mustard, soy sauce, cinnamon, cloves, and allspice. Bring to a simmer over medium heat, stirring until the sugar dissolves.
4. **Thicken Glaze (optional):** If you prefer a thicker glaze, mix cornstarch with a little water to make a slurry. Stir into the simmering glaze and cook until thickened.
5. **Glaze Ham:** Brush the glaze generously over the ham.
6. **Bake:** Bake the ham, basting with the glaze every 20-30 minutes, for about 1.5 to 2 hours, or until heated through and caramelized.
7. **Rest and Serve:** Let the ham rest for 10-15 minutes before slicing.

Enjoy your flavorful Coffee-Orange Glazed Ham!

Coffee-Infused Caramel Flan

Ingredients:

For the Caramel:

- 1 cup granulated sugar
- 1/4 cup water

For the Flan:

- 1 cup whole milk
- 1 cup heavy cream
- 1/2 cup brewed coffee (cooled)
- 1/2 cup granulated sugar
- 4 large eggs
- 1 tsp vanilla extract
- 1/4 tsp salt

Instructions:

1. **Prepare Caramel:**
   - In a saucepan, combine the sugar and water. Cook over medium heat, stirring occasionally, until the mixture turns a deep amber color. This should take about 10 minutes. Be careful not to burn the caramel.
   - Immediately pour the caramel into the bottom of each ramekin, swirling to coat the bottom evenly. Allow the caramel to harden as you prepare the flan.
2. **Prepare Flan Mixture:**
   - Preheat your oven to 325°F (165°C).
   - In a saucepan, heat the milk and heavy cream over medium heat until just simmering. Remove from heat.
   - In a bowl, whisk together the sugar, eggs, vanilla extract, and salt until smooth.
   - Gradually whisk the hot milk mixture into the egg mixture. Add the brewed coffee and mix well.
3. **Assemble Flan:**
   - Strain the flan mixture through a fine-mesh sieve into a large bowl or measuring cup to ensure a smooth texture.
   - Pour the mixture over the hardened caramel in each ramekin.
4. **Bake:**
   - Place the ramekins in a baking dish and fill the dish with hot water halfway up the sides of the ramekins to create a water bath.
   - Bake for 45-55 minutes, or until the flan is set and a knife inserted into the center comes out clean.
5. **Cool and Serve:**

- Remove the ramekins from the water bath and let them cool to room temperature. Refrigerate for at least 4 hours or overnight.
- To serve, run a knife around the edges of each flan and invert onto a plate.

Enjoy your creamy and coffee-infused caramel flan!

Espresso-Infused Soufflé

Ingredients:

For the Soufflé Base:

- 1/2 cup brewed espresso (cooled)
- 1/4 cup granulated sugar
- 2 tbsp unsalted butter
- 2 tbsp all-purpose flour
- 1/2 cup whole milk
- 3 large egg yolks
- 1/2 tsp vanilla extract
- 1/4 tsp salt

For the Meringue:

- 3 large egg whites
- 1/4 tsp cream of tartar
- 1/4 cup granulated sugar

For Greasing and Coating:

- 1 tbsp unsalted butter (for greasing)
- 2 tbsp granulated sugar (for coating)

Instructions:

1. **Preheat Oven:** Preheat your oven to 375°F (190°C). Butter the inside of four ramekins and coat with granulated sugar, tapping out any excess.
2. **Prepare Soufflé Base:**
    - In a saucepan, melt the butter over medium heat. Stir in the flour and cook for about 1 minute to form a roux.
    - Gradually whisk in the milk and continue to cook until the mixture thickens and is smooth.
    - Remove from heat and whisk in the espresso, granulated sugar, egg yolks, vanilla extract, and salt until well combined. Set aside to cool slightly.
3. **Prepare Meringue:**
    - In a clean bowl, beat the egg whites and cream of tartar with an electric mixer until soft peaks form.
    - Gradually add the granulated sugar, continuing to beat until stiff peaks form and the meringue is glossy.
4. **Combine and Fold:**

- Gently fold the meringue into the espresso base mixture in thirds. Be careful not to deflate the meringue; fold until just combined.
5. **Fill Ramekins:**
    - Spoon the soufflé mixture into the prepared ramekins, filling them just below the rim. Smooth the tops with a spatula.
6. **Bake:**
    - Place the ramekins on a baking sheet and bake for 15-20 minutes, or until the soufflés are puffed and golden brown. Do not open the oven door during baking.
7. **Serve Immediately:**
    - Serve the soufflés right out of the oven as they will start to deflate quickly.

Enjoy your light and airy Espresso-Infused Soufflés!

Coffee-Scented Rice Pudding

Ingredients:

- 1/2 cup short-grain rice
- 2 cups milk
- 1/2 cup sugar
- 1/4 cup strong brewed coffee (cooled)
- 1/2 tsp vanilla extract
- 1/4 tsp ground cinnamon
- Pinch of salt

Instructions:

1. In a medium saucepan, combine rice, milk, sugar, and salt. Bring to a simmer over medium heat.
2. Reduce heat to low, cover, and cook for about 20-25 minutes, stirring occasionally, until rice is tender and mixture is creamy.
3. Stir in brewed coffee, vanilla extract, and cinnamon.
4. Cook for an additional 5 minutes, stirring constantly, until the pudding thickens slightly.
5. Remove from heat and let it cool. Serve warm or chilled. Enjoy!

Coffee-Scented Rice Pudding

Ingredients:

- 1/2 cup Arborio rice
- 2 cups whole milk
- 1/2 cup sugar
- 1/2 cup strong brewed coffee (cooled)
- 1/4 cup heavy cream
- 1/2 tsp vanilla extract
- 1/4 tsp ground cinnamon
- Pinch of salt

Instructions:

1. In a saucepan, combine milk, sugar, and salt. Heat over medium heat until warm.
2. Stir in the Arborio rice and reduce heat to low. Simmer, stirring occasionally, until the rice is tender and the mixture is creamy, about 25-30 minutes.
3. Stir in the brewed coffee, heavy cream, vanilla extract, and cinnamon. Cook for an additional 5 minutes, stirring frequently.
4. Remove from heat and let cool slightly before serving. Enjoy warm or chilled!

Almond Coffee Cake

Ingredients:

For the Cake:

- 1 cup (2 sticks) unsalted butter, softened
- 1 cup granulated sugar
- 2 large eggs
- 1 cup sour cream
- 1 teaspoon vanilla extract
- 2 cups all-purpose flour
- 1 1/2 teaspoons baking powder
- 1/2 teaspoon baking soda
- 1/4 teaspoon salt

For the Almond Filling:

- 1/2 cup packed brown sugar
- 1/2 cup sliced almonds
- 1/2 teaspoon ground cinnamon

For the Glaze (optional):

- 1/2 cup powdered sugar
- 1-2 tablespoons milk
- 1/4 teaspoon almond extract

Instructions:

1. **Preheat Oven:** Preheat your oven to 350°F (175°C). Grease and flour a 9-inch round cake pan or a 9x9-inch square baking pan.
2. **Prepare the Cake Batter:** In a large bowl, cream together the softened butter and granulated sugar until light and fluffy. Beat in the eggs, one at a time. Mix in the sour cream and vanilla extract.
3. **Combine Dry Ingredients:** In another bowl, whisk together the flour, baking powder, baking soda, and salt. Gradually add the dry ingredients to the creamed mixture, mixing until just combined.
4. **Prepare the Almond Filling:** In a small bowl, combine the brown sugar, sliced almonds, and ground cinnamon.
5. **Assemble the Cake:** Spread half of the cake batter evenly in the prepared pan. Sprinkle half of the almond filling mixture over the batter. Spread the remaining batter on top and sprinkle with the remaining almond filling.

6. **Bake:** Bake for 35-40 minutes, or until a toothpick inserted into the center comes out clean.
7. **Prepare the Glaze (Optional):** While the cake is cooling, mix together the powdered sugar, milk, and almond extract to make a glaze. Adjust the consistency with more milk or powdered sugar as needed.
8. **Cool and Glaze:** Let the cake cool in the pan for about 10 minutes before transferring it to a wire rack to cool completely. Drizzle with the almond glaze, if using.

Enjoy your Almond Coffee Cake with a cup of coffee or tea!

Coffee and Brown Sugar Granola

Ingredients:

- 3 cups old-fashioned rolled oats
- 1 cup nuts and seeds (such as almonds, walnuts, or sunflower seeds)
- 1/2 cup brown sugar
- 1/4 cup finely ground coffee (cooled)
- 1/2 cup honey or maple syrup
- 1/4 cup coconut oil or vegetable oil
- 1/2 tsp vanilla extract
- 1/2 tsp ground cinnamon
- 1/4 tsp salt
- 1/2 cup dried fruit (optional, such as cranberries, raisins, or apricots)

Instructions:

1. **Preheat Oven:** Preheat your oven to 350°F (175°C). Line a large baking sheet with parchment paper or a silicone baking mat.
2. **Mix Dry Ingredients:** In a large bowl, combine the oats, nuts and seeds, brown sugar, coffee grounds, ground cinnamon, and salt.
3. **Combine Wet Ingredients:** In a small saucepan, heat the honey (or maple syrup) and coconut oil over medium heat until melted and combined. Remove from heat and stir in the vanilla extract.
4. **Combine Wet and Dry Ingredients:** Pour the wet ingredients over the dry mixture and stir well to ensure everything is evenly coated.
5. **Bake:** Spread the mixture evenly on the prepared baking sheet. Bake for 20-25 minutes, stirring halfway through, until the granola is golden brown and crisp.
6. **Cool and Add Dried Fruit:** Allow the granola to cool completely on the baking sheet (it will become crispier as it cools). If using, stir in the dried fruit after cooling.
7. **Store:** Store the granola in an airtight container at room temperature for up to 2 weeks.

Enjoy your Coffee and Brown Sugar Granola with yogurt, milk, or just as a crunchy snack!

Coffee-Infused Beef Stew

Ingredients:

- 2 lbs beef chuck, cut into 1-inch cubes
- 2 tbsp olive oil
- 1 large onion, chopped
- 3 cloves garlic, minced
- 3 tbsp tomato paste
- 1 cup strong brewed coffee (cooled)
- 2 cups beef broth
- 1 cup red wine (optional, can substitute with more beef broth)
- 3 carrots, peeled and cut into chunks
- 2 celery stalks, chopped
- 3 large potatoes, peeled and cubed
- 1 bay leaf
- 1 tsp dried thyme
- 1 tsp dried rosemary
- Salt and freshly ground black pepper, to taste
- 1 tbsp all-purpose flour (optional, for thickening)
- 2 tbsp chopped fresh parsley (for garnish, optional)

Instructions:

1. **Brown the Beef:** In a large pot or Dutch oven, heat olive oil over medium-high heat. Add the beef cubes in batches, searing them until browned on all sides. Remove the beef and set aside.
2. **Sauté Aromatics:** In the same pot, add chopped onion and cook until softened, about 5 minutes. Add minced garlic and cook for another minute.
3. **Add Tomato Paste:** Stir in the tomato paste and cook for 2 minutes to caramelize slightly.
4. **Deglaze with Coffee:** Pour in the brewed coffee, stirring to deglaze the pot and scrape up any browned bits from the bottom.
5. **Add Liquids and Seasonings:** Return the browned beef to the pot. Add beef broth and red wine (if using). Stir in bay leaf, thyme, rosemary, salt, and pepper.
6. **Simmer:** Bring to a boil, then reduce heat to low. Cover and simmer for about 1.5 to 2 hours, or until the beef is tender.
7. **Add Vegetables:** Add carrots, celery, and potatoes. Continue to simmer for an additional 30-40 minutes, or until the vegetables are tender.
8. **Thicken the Stew (Optional):** If you prefer a thicker stew, mix 1 tablespoon of flour with a little water to create a slurry. Stir the slurry into the stew and cook for an additional 10 minutes until thickened.
9. **Adjust Seasoning:** Taste and adjust seasoning with more salt and pepper if needed.

10. **Garnish and Serve:** Remove the bay leaf. Garnish with chopped fresh parsley if desired. Serve hot with crusty bread or over rice.

Enjoy the rich, complex flavors of this coffee-infused beef stew!

Coffee Almond Ice Cream

Ingredients:

- 1 cup whole milk
- 1 cup heavy cream
- 1/2 cup granulated sugar
- 1/2 cup strong brewed coffee (cooled)
- 1/4 cup almond butter
- 1 tsp vanilla extract
- 1/2 cup chopped toasted almonds

Instructions:

1. **Combine Ingredients:** In a bowl, whisk together milk, cream, sugar, coffee, almond butter, and vanilla extract until the sugar is dissolved and the almond butter is well blended.
2. **Chill Mixture:** Refrigerate the mixture for at least 2 hours, or until well chilled.
3. **Churn:** Pour the chilled mixture into an ice cream maker and churn according to the manufacturer's instructions, usually for about 20-25 minutes.
4. **Add Almonds:** During the last few minutes of churning, add the chopped toasted almonds.
5. **Freeze:** Transfer the ice cream to a lidded container and freeze for at least 2 hours to firm up.
6. **Serve:** Scoop and enjoy your Coffee Almond Ice Cream!

This ice cream combines the rich flavors of coffee and almond for a delicious treat.

Affogato Cheesecake

Ingredients:

For the Crust:

- 1 1/2 cups graham cracker crumbs
- 1/4 cup sugar
- 1/2 cup melted butter

For the Filling:

- 4 (8 oz each) packages cream cheese, softened
- 1 cup granulated sugar
- 1 cup sour cream
- 1 tsp vanilla extract
- 4 large eggs
- 1 cup heavy cream
- 1/4 cup strong brewed coffee (cooled)

For the Topping:

- 1/2 cup strong brewed coffee
- 1/4 cup sugar (optional, adjust to taste)
- Whipped cream, for garnish

Instructions:

1. **Preheat Oven:** Preheat your oven to 325°F (160°C). Grease a 9-inch springform pan.
2. **Prepare the Crust:** In a bowl, mix graham cracker crumbs, sugar, and melted butter. Press the mixture evenly into the bottom of the prepared pan. Bake for 10 minutes, then cool.
3. **Prepare the Filling:** Beat the cream cheese until smooth. Gradually add sugar and beat until creamy. Mix in sour cream and vanilla extract. Add eggs one at a time, beating well after each addition.
4. **Add Coffee:** Mix the brewed coffee into the filling until combined. Pour the batter over the cooled crust.
5. **Bake:** Bake for 55-65 minutes, or until the center is set and the edges are slightly puffed. Turn off the oven and let the cheesecake cool inside with the door slightly open for 1 hour.
6. **Chill:** Refrigerate the cheesecake for at least 4 hours or overnight.
7. **Prepare the Topping:** In a small saucepan, heat the brewed coffee and sugar (if using) until the sugar dissolves. Allow to cool.

8. **Serve:** Before serving, drizzle the cooled coffee topping over the cheesecake and garnish with whipped cream.

Enjoy the indulgent blend of creamy cheesecake and rich coffee flavor!

Mocha Bread Pudding

Ingredients:

- 6 cups cubed day-old bread (such as brioche or challah)
- 2 cups whole milk
- 1 cup heavy cream
- 1 cup granulated sugar
- 1/2 cup strong brewed coffee (cooled)
- 1/2 cup semi-sweet chocolate chips
- 4 large eggs
- 1 tsp vanilla extract
- 1/4 cup cocoa powder
- 1/2 tsp ground cinnamon
- Pinch of salt

Instructions:

1. **Preheat Oven:** Preheat your oven to 350°F (175°C). Grease a 9x13-inch baking dish.
2. **Prepare Bread:** Place the cubed bread in the greased baking dish.
3. **Make the Custard:** In a large bowl, whisk together the milk, cream, sugar, coffee, eggs, vanilla extract, cocoa powder, cinnamon, and salt until well combined. Stir in the chocolate chips.
4. **Combine:** Pour the custard mixture evenly over the bread cubes. Press down gently to ensure all bread is soaked. Let it sit for 15-20 minutes to absorb.
5. **Bake:** Bake for 45-50 minutes, or until the pudding is set and the top is golden brown.
6. **Cool and Serve:** Let it cool slightly before serving. Optional: Serve warm with a drizzle of chocolate sauce or a dollop of whipped cream.

Enjoy the rich and comforting flavors of mocha in this bread pudding!

Coffee-Maple Syrup

Ingredients:

- 1 cup pure maple syrup
- 1/4 cup strong brewed coffee (cooled)
- 1/2 tsp vanilla extract (optional)

Instructions:

1. **Combine Ingredients:** In a small saucepan, combine the maple syrup and brewed coffee.
2. **Heat:** Heat over medium heat until warmed through, stirring occasionally.
3. **Add Vanilla (Optional):** If using, stir in the vanilla extract once the syrup is heated.
4. **Serve:** Pour over pancakes, waffles, or French toast.

Enjoy the rich, aromatic blend of coffee and maple!

Coffee-Walnut Brownies

Ingredients:

For the Brownies:

- 1/2 cup (1 stick) unsalted butter
- 1 cup granulated sugar
- 1/4 cup strong brewed coffee (cooled)
- 2 large eggs
- 1 tsp vanilla extract
- 1/2 cup unsweetened cocoa powder
- 1/2 cup all-purpose flour
- 1/4 tsp salt
- 1/4 tsp baking powder
- 1/2 cup chopped walnuts

For the Coffee Glaze (Optional):

- 1/2 cup powdered sugar
- 2-3 tbsp brewed coffee (cooled)
- 1/4 tsp vanilla extract

Instructions:

1. **Preheat Oven:** Preheat your oven to 350°F (175°C). Grease or line an 8x8-inch baking pan with parchment paper.
2. **Melt Butter:** In a medium saucepan, melt the butter over low heat. Remove from heat and stir in the granulated sugar and cooled coffee.
3. **Add Eggs and Vanilla:** Beat in the eggs one at a time, then stir in the vanilla extract.
4. **Combine Dry Ingredients:** In a separate bowl, whisk together cocoa powder, flour, salt, and baking powder.
5. **Mix Wet and Dry Ingredients:** Gradually add the dry ingredients to the wet mixture, stirring until just combined. Fold in the chopped walnuts.
6. **Bake:** Pour the batter into the prepared pan and spread it evenly. Bake for 25-30 minutes, or until a toothpick inserted into the center comes out with a few moist crumbs.
7. **Cool:** Allow the brownies to cool in the pan on a wire rack before cutting into squares.
8. **Prepare Coffee Glaze (Optional):** In a small bowl, whisk together powdered sugar, brewed coffee, and vanilla extract until smooth. Drizzle over cooled brownies if desired.

Enjoy the rich combination of coffee and chocolate with a satisfying crunch from the walnuts!

Espresso Trifle

Ingredients:

For the Espresso Soaked Cake:

- 1 cup brewed espresso or strong coffee (cooled)
- 1 store-bought or homemade pound cake (cut into cubes)

For the Mascarpone Cream:

- 1 cup heavy cream
- 1/2 cup mascarpone cheese
- 1/4 cup granulated sugar
- 1 tsp vanilla extract

For the Coffee Syrup:

- 1/4 cup brewed espresso or strong coffee
- 2 tbsp coffee liqueur (optional)

For Assembly:

- 1/4 cup chocolate shavings or cocoa powder
- Fresh berries or shaved chocolate for garnish (optional)

Instructions:

1. **Prepare Coffee Syrup:** In a small bowl, mix together the brewed espresso and coffee liqueur (if using). Set aside.
2. **Soak the Cake:** Dip the pound cake cubes into the coffee syrup briefly, just enough to soak them without becoming too soggy.
3. **Make the Mascarpone Cream:** In a large bowl, beat the heavy cream until soft peaks form. In another bowl, mix mascarpone cheese, sugar, and vanilla extract until smooth. Gently fold the mascarpone mixture into the whipped cream until combined.
4. **Assemble the Trifle:** In a trifle dish or individual serving glasses, layer half of the soaked cake cubes, then half of the mascarpone cream. Repeat with the remaining cake cubes and mascarpone cream.
5. **Chill:** Refrigerate for at least 2 hours to allow flavors to meld.
6. **Garnish and Serve:** Before serving, top with chocolate shavings or a dusting of cocoa powder. Garnish with fresh berries or additional shaved chocolate if desired.

Enjoy this luxurious and coffee-flavored dessert!

Coffee-Glazed Chicken Wings

Ingredients:

For the Glaze:

- 1/2 cup strong brewed coffee (cooled)
- 1/4 cup brown sugar
- 1/4 cup soy sauce
- 2 tbsp balsamic vinegar
- 2 tbsp honey
- 1 tbsp minced garlic
- 1 tsp grated ginger
- 1/2 tsp black pepper

For the Chicken Wings:

- 2 lbs chicken wings
- 1 tbsp olive oil
- Salt and pepper, to taste

Instructions:

1. **Preheat Oven:** Preheat your oven to 400°F (200°C). Line a baking sheet with parchment paper or a silicone mat.
2. **Prepare Chicken Wings:** Pat the chicken wings dry with paper towels. Toss with olive oil, salt, and pepper. Arrange in a single layer on the prepared baking sheet.
3. **Bake Wings:** Bake the wings for 35-40 minutes, or until they are crispy and golden brown, flipping halfway through.
4. **Make the Glaze:** While the wings are baking, combine the brewed coffee, brown sugar, soy sauce, balsamic vinegar, honey, garlic, ginger, and black pepper in a saucepan. Bring to a simmer over medium heat and cook until the glaze has thickened slightly, about 10 minutes.
5. **Glaze the Wings:** Remove the wings from the oven and brush them generously with the coffee glaze. Return to the oven and bake for an additional 5 minutes to set the glaze.
6. **Serve:** Serve the wings hot, drizzled with any remaining glaze.

Enjoy the rich, smoky flavor of these Coffee-Glazed Chicken Wings!

Mocha Buttercream Frosting

Ingredients:

- 1 cup (2 sticks) unsalted butter, softened
- 3 cups powdered sugar
- 1/4 cup unsweetened cocoa powder
- 2 tbsp strong brewed coffee (cooled)
- 2 tbsp heavy cream
- 1 tsp vanilla extract
- A pinch of salt (optional)

Instructions:

1. **Beat the Butter:** In a large bowl, beat the softened butter with an electric mixer on medium speed until creamy and smooth.
2. **Add Dry Ingredients:** Gradually add the powdered sugar and cocoa powder, beating on low speed until combined. Increase speed to medium and continue beating until light and fluffy.
3. **Add Coffee and Cream:** Mix in the brewed coffee, heavy cream, and vanilla extract. Beat on medium speed until fully incorporated and the frosting is smooth.
4. **Adjust Consistency:** If the frosting is too thick, add more heavy cream, one tablespoon at a time, until you reach your desired consistency. If it's too thin, add a little more powdered sugar.
5. **Add Salt (Optional):** Taste the frosting and add a pinch of salt if needed to enhance the flavors.
6. **Frost Your Cake:** Use the frosting to decorate your cake or cupcakes as desired.

Enjoy this rich, coffee-infused buttercream frosting on your favorite baked goods!

Espresso Chocolate Sauce

Ingredients:

- 1/2 cup heavy cream
- 1/2 cup espresso or strong brewed coffee
- 1 cup semi-sweet chocolate chips
- 2 tbsp unsalted butter
- 1/4 cup granulated sugar (optional, adjust to taste)
- 1/2 tsp vanilla extract

Instructions:

1. **Heat Cream and Coffee:** In a small saucepan, heat the heavy cream and espresso over medium heat until it starts to simmer.
2. **Add Chocolate and Sugar:** Remove from heat and stir in the chocolate chips and sugar (if using) until the chocolate is fully melted and smooth.
3. **Add Butter and Vanilla:** Stir in the butter and vanilla extract until the sauce is glossy and well combined.
4. **Cool and Store:** Allow the sauce to cool slightly before using. It will thicken as it cools. Store any leftovers in an airtight container in the refrigerator for up to 2 weeks. Reheat gently before using.

Drizzle this decadent sauce over ice cream, pancakes, or desserts for a delightful coffee-chocolate flavor!

Coffee Smoothie

Ingredients:

- 1 cup brewed coffee (cooled)
- 1 banana
- 1/2 cup Greek yogurt (plain or vanilla)
- 1/4 cup milk (any kind)
- 1 tbsp honey or maple syrup (adjust to taste)
- 1/2 tsp vanilla extract
- Ice cubes (optional, for a colder smoothie)

Instructions:

1. **Blend Ingredients:** In a blender, combine the cooled coffee, banana, Greek yogurt, milk, honey (or maple syrup), and vanilla extract.
2. **Add Ice:** If you want a colder, thicker smoothie, add a handful of ice cubes.
3. **Blend:** Blend until smooth and creamy.
4. **Serve:** Pour into a glass and enjoy immediately.

This Coffee Smoothie is a perfect pick-me-up for any time of day!

www.ingramcontent.com/pod-product-compliance
Lightning Source LLC
LaVergne TN
LVHW081319060526
838201LV00055B/2361